The Box Hill Book
of
Bugs
and other small creatures

Anne and John Bebbington

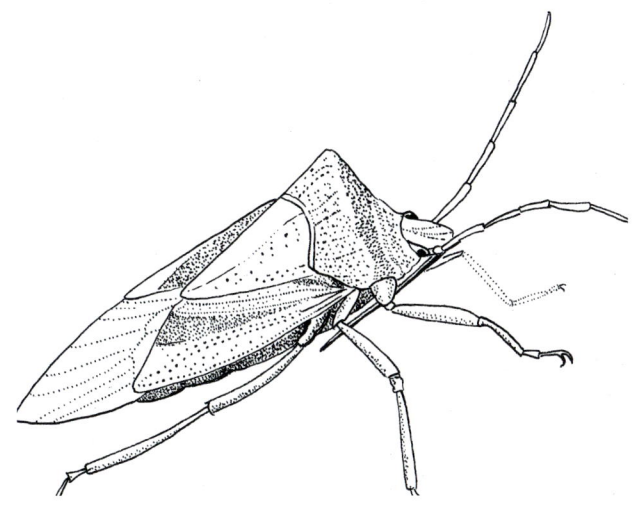

The Friends of Box Hill
2003

Dr Anne Bebbington trained as a botanist, specialising in bryophyte ecology and **John Bebbington FRPS** trained as an agricultural zoologist. They joined the Field Studies Council in 1970, working at first in North Wales, then moving to Juniper Hall in 1978. Anne is now a Senior Teaching Officer and John is Head of Centre at Juniper Hall, where they teach at all levels from Primary to third-level University, postgraduate, in-service teacher training and Leisure and Professional Development courses for adults.

Anne specialises in plant science and plant ecology and has a particular interest in both botanical and invertebrate illustration. John is especially interested in close-up and macro photography and in 1991 was awarded Fellowship of the Royal Photographic Society for a panel of slides on insect colouration.

Both Anne and John have always been keen naturalists and combine their illustrative and photographic skills with their teaching. They have contributed to a wide range of publications and produced a number of identification guides and other fold-out charts aimed at children and adults with no scientific background. For more information see **www.bebbingtonsnaturepix.co.uk**

Acknowledgements

We would like to thank The Friends of Box Hill for supporting and funding this book, and especially Sandra Wedgwood; Sue Tatham for her hard work and expertise in the design and preparation of the text; Stephanie Randall for proof reading and Andrew Tatham who prepared the map and the colour plates.

COVER PHOTOGRAPHS
Front cover: Nettle weevil *Phyllobius urticae* [p35]
Back cover: Hoverfly *Episyrphus balteatus* [p31] on flowerhead of Wild parsnip
TITLE PAGE DRAWING
Hawthorn shieldbug *Acanthosoma haemorrhoidale* [p18]

Copyright © 2003   Text by Dr Anne Bebbington and John Bebbington FRPS
with photographs by John Bebbington FRPS
and line drawings by Dr Anne Bebbington

Published by The Friends of Box Hill, Pixham Mill, Dorking, Surrey RH4 1PQ
ISBN 0 9534430 5 1   Print managed by Centurion Press Ltd

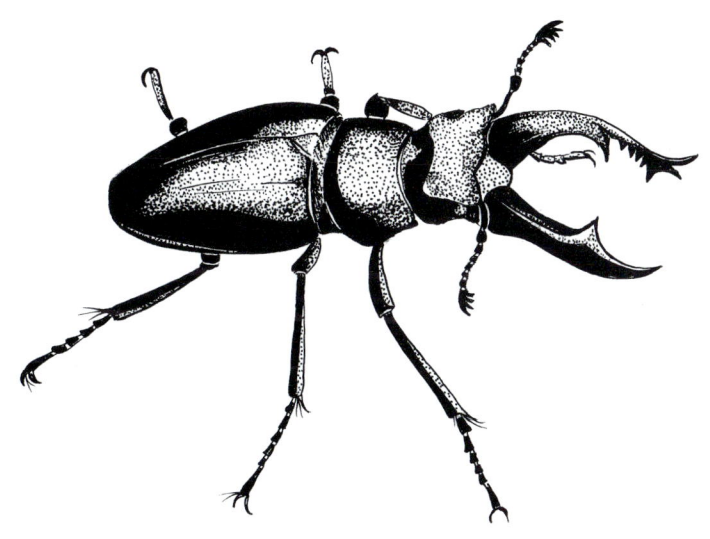

CONTENTS

What is an invertebrate?
The choice of animals
The arrangement of animals in this book
Conservation
Why is Box Hill such a good place for invertebrates?
Animal descriptions
Further reading
Map of Box Hill

Introduction

Walking on Box Hill you will notice an enormous number and variety of small creatures (often loosely referred to as 'bugs'). These animals all belong to a major subdivision of the animal kingdom called the **invertebrates.**

What is an invertebrate?

The animal kingdom can conveniently be divided into two major groups – the vertebrates and the invertebrates. The five major groups of vertebrates, the fishes, amphibians, reptiles, birds and mammals, all have an internal skeleton which includes a backbone. This backbone consists of small bones called vertebrae from which the vertebrates get their name.

Many invertebrates have no skeleton at all. Some have an exoskeleton – a hard jointed external skeleton, like a suit of armour, at least in the adult stage. None of them has a backbone, hence invertebrates.

Most of us are familiar with animals belonging to the five major groups of vertebrates but it may come as a surprise to find that the number of different kinds of invertebrates far exceeds the number of kinds of vertebrates. More than 98% of the world's known kinds of animals are invertebrates – around 1,015,000 different kinds have been described so far as against only around 48,000 vertebrates, and more are still being discovered.

The animal kingdom is divided into a number of major groups called phyla (singular phylum). These are the largest groupings and are themselves split up into increasingly smaller groups as follows, using the stag beetle as an example:

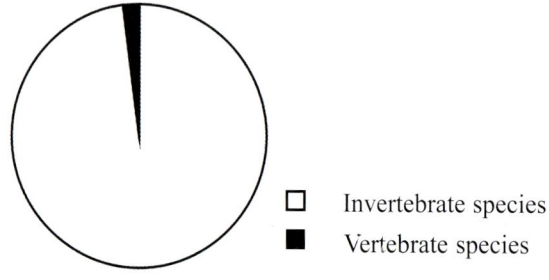

□ Invertebrate species
■ Vertebrate species

Known numbers of different kinds of vertebrates and invertebrates in the world fauna

Phylum Arthropoda
Class Insecta
Order Coleoptera
Family Lucanidae
Genus *Lucanus*
Species *cervus*

Common name Stag beetle
Scientific name *Lucanus cervus*

Although there are many invertebrate phyla represented on Box Hill, most of the invertebrates you will find belong to the following three:
- Phylum **Annelida** which includes worms
- Phylum **Mollusca** which includes slugs and snails
- Phylum **Arthropoda** which includes insects, spiders and their allies, woodlice, centipedes and millipedes.

The choice of animals

So many different kinds of invertebrates are found on Box Hill that it is impossible to do anything other than to make a personal selection based on the twenty-five years which the authors have spent at Juniper Hall Field Centre, walking and teaching on the Hill.

Within each of the three phyla named above we have chosen a few representatives which have special links with Box Hill, have an interesting story attached to them, or are likely to be easily seen while you are out walking. This includes adult insects whose young stages live in freshwater, but not the young stages themselves, or other freshwater invertebrates.

The aims of this book are to help you to find out which group of invertebrates an animal you have found belongs to, to give you more information about that group of animals, and to highlight the animals which you are most likely to encounter.

There are also references to more detailed publications which can help you to develop your interest and pursue it further.

The arrangement of animals in this book

For simplicity we have used the number of legs which the adults have to help the reader to find out which phylum or major group an animal belongs to. This is far from being a scientific approach but it is logical.

Conservation

It is very important to conserve the high biodiversity of this very special area. Please do not collect animals. Observe them carefully, make notes, draw or photograph them. Treat all animals with great care when examining them and return them to their natural habitat as soon as possible. If you turn over logs or stones make sure that you return them carefully to their original position.

Why is Box Hill such a good place for invertebrates?

The Box Hill estate has a wide range of habitats including species-rich chalk grassland, scrub and wood-land on chalk soil. Grassland, scrub and woodland are also to be found on the acidic clay-with-flints cap on the top of the downs, while along the river are damp meadows and woodlands. The estate also includes and is partly bordered by agricultural land.

The major aim of management by the National Trust is to create a rich diversity of microhabitats within each habitat type, creating a diversity of vegetation which is essential for invertebrate diversity.

Thus, on the grassland, fertilisers are not used and grazing is carried out by primitive breeds of sheep, by highland cattle and other livestock which are neither given supplementary feeds nor treated with broad-spectrum antibiotics. This means that the dung which is produced is simply returning nutrients which originate in the soil. This provides a rich habitat for a wide range of invertebrates such as flies and dung beetles and their parasites and predators; in turn these are eaten by birds and bats.

In many areas scrub is only partly cleared, providing habitats transitional between grassland and woodland. In woodlands thinning and coppicing are carried out and dead wood is often left either where it has fallen or stacked in log piles, providing habitats for wood-boring insects such as Stag beetles and shelter for other invertebrates.

In addition the almost continental climate of southeastern England encourages some nationally rare species.

Stag beetle larva — lives in dead wood

Animals whose adults have no legs

WORMS

(phylum *Annelida* class *Oligochaeta*)

Worms have a segmented body with large numbers of segments (note that the larvae of some insects have no legs; they all however have less than 20 body segments). On each segment are microscopic bristles (chaetae). A worm moves by gripping the sides of its burrow with the chaetae on the hind segments, extending the front segments forwards, then gripping the sides of the burrow with the chaetae on the front segments and pulling the hind part of the body forward.

About one-third of the way down the body you will notice a smooth, slightly swollen 'saddle'. Each worm is hermaphrodite (having both male and female sex organs). This can be an advantage, especially to animals which lead a relatively sedentary life providing few contacts between individuals. It enables two exchanges of sperm and egg laying by both partners instead of just one at each meeting of two individuals. When mating, two worms lie side by side, head-to-tail, joined at the saddles. Eggs are laid in a small cocoon in the soil.

The nervous system of the worm is concentrated in the 'head' end and, if the worm is damaged, this is the part which is most likely to survive. The head and tail ends of the worm also have light-sensitive cells (either end may protrude from the tunnel at night when worms are most active on or near the surface).

There are many different kinds of worms living in soil, leaf litter and dead wood. In loose damp soil they burrow by forcing their way between soil particles but in compacted soil they will eat soil to create a burrow. They are extremely important because they mix and aerate the soil. They also help to incorporate dead plant material by pulling it down into their burrows where it is fragmented and eaten. Together with excreted material and other secretions from the worms this helps to enrich the soil.

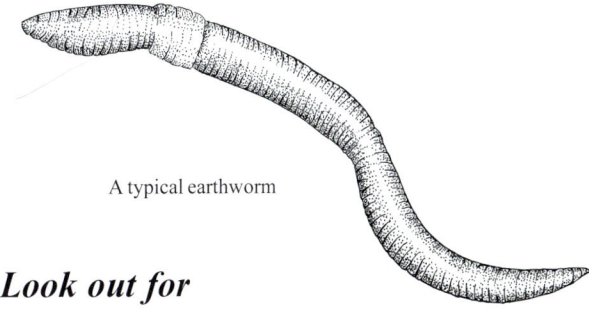

A typical earthworm

Look out for

Worm casts, which can be very numerous, on the short grassland on Juniper Top or the Burford Spur - these are a mixture of soil and minute fragments of plant material.

Worms on the surface of footpaths or leaf litter in woodland in wet weather.

MOLLUSCS
(phylum *Mollusca* class *Gastropoda*)

Snails and slugs can readily be distinguished from worms and insect larvae by their unsegmented body and the presence of tentacles. The distinction between slugs and snails however is less clear. Snails all have a coiled shell which in many species is large enough to retreat into. In a few however the shell is very small in relation to the body. Those species referred to as 'slugs' appear to have lost their external shell but a few have a very small one. There is a small shell inside most species.

Slugs and snails move along by waves of muscular contraction on the sole of the foot which is lubricated by mucus, leaving a characteristic slime trail as the animal moves forward. In many the front of the head is armed with two pairs of tentacles, the upper pair bearing eyespots at the tip. In the more primitive species there is only one pair of tentacles with eye spots at the base. Snails and slugs feed using a tongue or *radula* covered with thousands of tiny rasping teeth and a horny upper jaw. While most slugs and snails feed on algae, lichens, fungi and rotting vegetation, many eat carrion and a few (such as the group to which the Garlic snail belongs) are carnivorous, eating other snails and their eggs.

SNAILS

Most of our British land snails belong to the order *Pulmonata* and have lungs. However a few (order *Prosobranchia*) are less well adapted to life on dry land and still use gills for respiration. These also have a horny plate, the operculum, with which they can close their shell and help to preserve moisture.

Look out for

The Edible or **Roman snail** *Helix pomatia* [inside front cover] which is confined to the chalk of southern England and needs high calcium carbonate levels for its thick shell. It is the largest north-west European snail, taking five years or more to grow to maturity. It appears in April after hibernating in the soil, and in late spring you may see these snails performing an elaborate 'courtship dance', entwined and swaying slowly from side to side as they mate. Each snail is in fact hermaphrodite (both male and female). Later, in summer, eggs are laid in the soil in a shaded damp place and the adults die. You will find many empty shells lying around in places such as Juniper Bottom. Young Roman snails hibernate in the soil and seal their shell with a white plate made mostly of calcium carbonate. This snail is protected on Box Hill.

Banded snails [inside front cover] which are often seen in large numbers on damp days, or may be found climbing tree trunks or tall vegetation in dry weather. There are two species commonly found on the Hill, which are hard to separate as juveniles but can be distinguished by the lip of the shell as adults: the white-lipped *Helix hortensis* and the black-lipped *Helix nemoralis*. Both have a wide range of colour forms, varying from pale yellow or orange without stripes to very heavily banded and in some cases almost black. If you look carefully you may find piles of empty broken snail shells – thrushes' anvils – in open areas. If you find a pair of snails mating look for the love darts which they fire into each other. These contain stimulating chemicals which assist in mating.

The Garlic snail *Oxychilus alliarius* has a flat, very shiny shell and is found under logs and in leaf litter in woodland, for example in Ashurst Rough. The snail smells very strongly of garlic if handled - a defence against predators.

Tree snails (family *Clausilidae)* have a characteristic pointed shape, which is an adaptation for climbing and hiding in crevices, and may be found on tree trunks where they feed on algae.

A typical tree snail

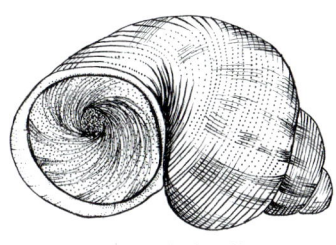

Round-mouthed snail with operculum closed

The Round-mouthed snail or **Land winkle** *Pomatias elegans* is an example of the gilled snails. Unlike the snails already described it has only two tentacles which are triangular and have an eyespot at their base. The shell can be closed by means of a hard horny plate, the operculum.

SLUGS

You are most likely to encounter our two largest species of slug on Box Hill in damp conditions.

Look out for

A large, very common slug *Arion ater* which varies in colour between black and brick-red. If annoyed, the slug will contract and rock from side to side. It is easy to see the lung-opening on this large species. You will probably know this slug as a serious garden pest but it has an important role to play on the Hill – it even eats wet paper and cardboard!

A very large, spotted slug - Leopard slug *Limax maximus* [inside front cover] often seen climbing trees in woodland. On smooth-barked trees such as Ash you may see 'feeding trails' where algae have been rasped off the bark.

7

Animals whose adults have six jointed legs

INSECTS (phylum *Arthropoda* class *Insecta*)

The next 15 groups of invertebrates all belong to the large and very diverse class **Insecta** (insects) - the most successful group of animals in the world.

In the typical insect the body is divided into a head, a thorax and an abdomen:

The head carries the main sensory organs and is the main nerve centre of the animal. It carries a pair of sensory organs called antennae which can take many forms. These are used primarily to detect food sources and potential mates. Eyes can be single-lensed simple eyes (ocelli) as in the juveniles, but in most adults the eyes are large and compound with many thousands of lenses. Many adults can perceive colour and pattern and use this facility in finding food and mates. Some adults have both simple and compound eyes (e.g. bugs, bees and wasps). The simple eyes appear to have an important regulatory role in the daily activity cycles, being involved in regulating daytime and night-time activity. Some adult insects have greatly reduced mouthparts and do not feed (e.g. Mayflies) but others have well developed biting or sucking mouthparts. Many insects also have segmented mouthparts called palps which carry chemosensitive cells, acting as the insect equivalent of taste buds.

The thorax is the heavily muscled section of the body which, at least in adults, carries 3 pairs of jointed legs. In some, one or more pairs may be adapted for special purposes, e.g. jumping in the grasshoppers. Wings, if present, will also be attached to the thorax. There are two pairs of wings, although one pair may be modified to form wing cases (beetles) or balancing organs (true flies).

The abdomen is usually clearly segmented and carries the digestive and reproductive organs. Some species may have tails (cerci) on the hind end of the abdomen.

Diagram of a generalised insect showing body parts

Insect Life Cycles

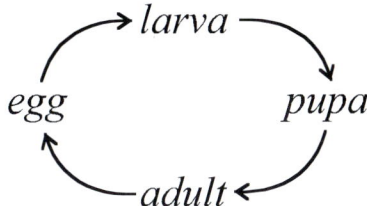

A complete (4-stage) life cycle

Many insects have a complete life cycle. The larva looks totally unlike the adult and passes through a resting pupal stage before the mature adult emerges. Butterflies, for example, have this sort of life cycle.

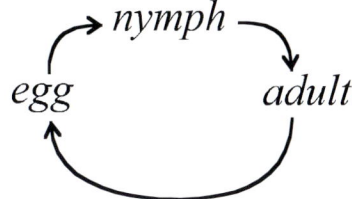

An incomplete (3-stage) life cycle

Other insects, such as the grasshoppers, have what is known as an incomplete life cycle. The egg hatches into a nymph which closely resembles the adult. As the insect grows and moults, its wings and reproductive organs mature, until at the final moult the fully mature adult is formed. There is no pupal resting stage.

SPRINGTAILS (order *Collembola*)

Most springtails are very small (<1mm) although some may reach 5mm. They are however extremely abundant. One scientist calculated that there were as many as 239 million in just one acre of meadowland. They feed on dead or dying plant material.

Look out for

Lucerne fleas (family *Sminthuridae*) tiny green insects, seen hopping about in meadows.

Fairly large species (5mm or so) **which are good jumpers** and belong to the genus *Tomocerus,* usually seen in leaf litter in the woodland. The springing organ is clipped to the underside of the abdomen when the animal is at rest. When it is released the animal is shot forward through the air.

A tomocerid Springtail

A KEY TO THE MAIN GROUPS OF COMMON INSECTS LIKELY TO BE FOUND ON BOX HILL

The following key will help you to identify the group which the insect you are looking at belongs to.

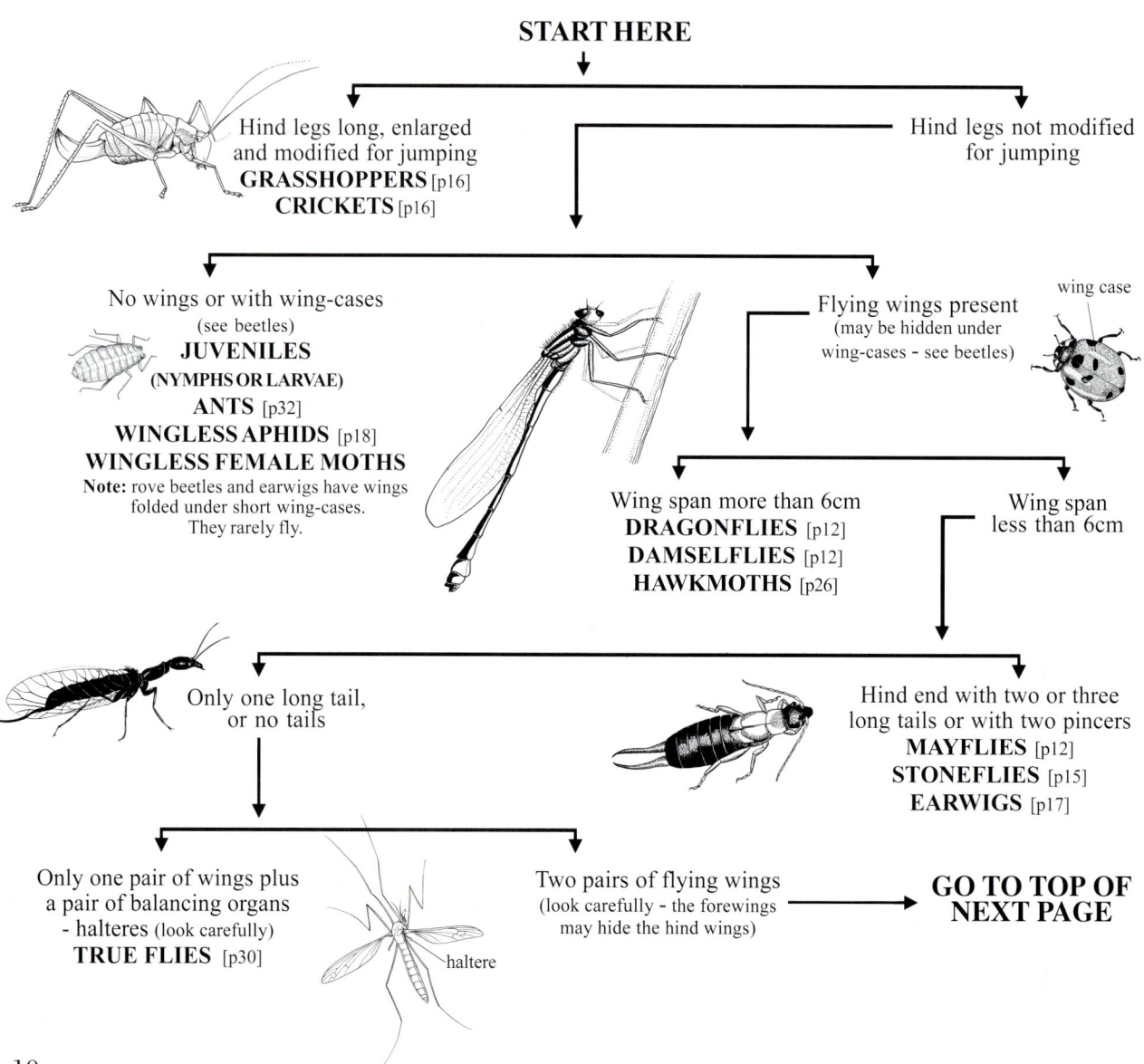

10

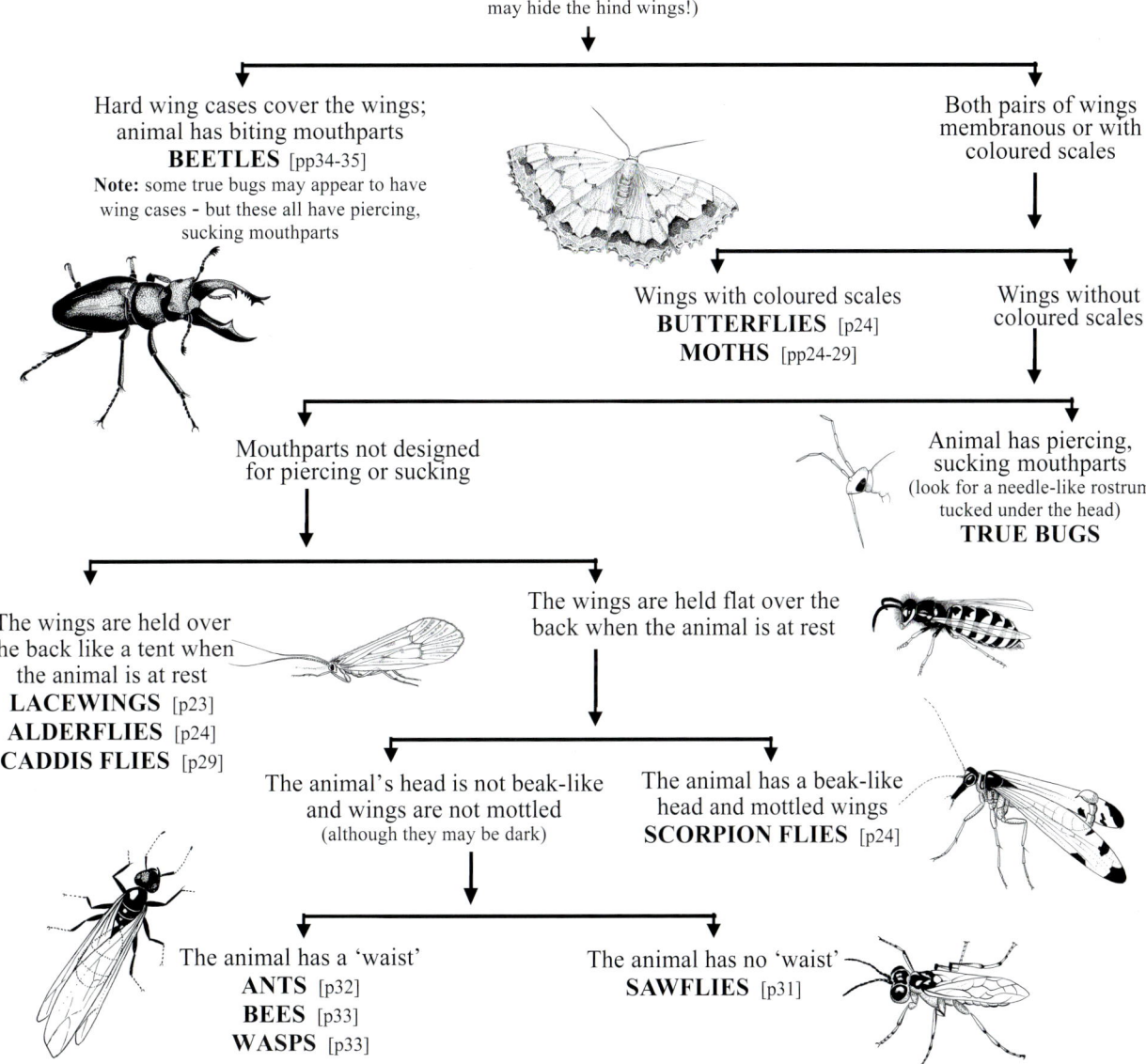

CONTINUE HERE
Two pairs of flying wings
(look carefully - the forewings may hide the hind wings!)

Hard wing cases cover the wings; animal has biting mouthparts
BEETLES [pp34-35]
Note: some true bugs may appear to have wing cases - but these all have piercing, sucking mouthparts

Both pairs of wings membranous or with coloured scales

Wings with coloured scales
BUTTERFLIES [p24]
MOTHS [pp24-29]

Wings without coloured scales

Animal has piercing, sucking mouthparts
(look for a needle-like rostrum tucked under the head)
TRUE BUGS

Mouthparts not designed for piercing or sucking

The wings are held over the back like a tent when the animal is at rest
LACEWINGS [p23]
ALDERFLIES [p24]
CADDIS FLIES [p29]

The wings are held flat over the back when the animal is at rest

The animal's head is not beak-like and wings are not mottled
(although they may be dark)

The animal has a beak-like head and mottled wings
SCORPION FLIES [p24]

The animal has a 'waist'
ANTS [p32]
BEES [p33]
WASPS [p33]

The animal has no 'waist'
SAWFLIES [p31]

11

MAYFLIES (order *Ephemeroptera*)

The scientific name refers to their short (ephemeral) adult life — most only live for a day during which time they do not feed. Most of the life of the mayfly is spent as a juvenile (nymph) in water feeding on algae or organic debris. A few are partly carnivorous. The adults can be recognised as delicate, weakly flying insects with two or three long tails.

Look out for

Large swarms of mayflies along the banks of the River Mole as they emerge from the water to mate and lay eggs.

The burrowing mayfly *Ephemera danica* [p13] the largest species, which can be found flying or resting on vegetation on the banks of the River Mole in May and June. It can be up to 3cm long including the tails.

DAMSELFLIES & DRAGONFLIES (order *Odonata*)

Like the mayflies, these insects have aquatic juveniles. Both of these groups of insects are hunters with excellent vision and have legs which are arranged for grabbing prey in midair.

Dragonflies are larger and more robust insects which rest with their wings held horizontally out from the body and have large compound eyes which appear to meet in the middle when viewed from above.

Most damselflies rest with their wings held vertically above the back and their eyes are clearly separated when viewed from above.

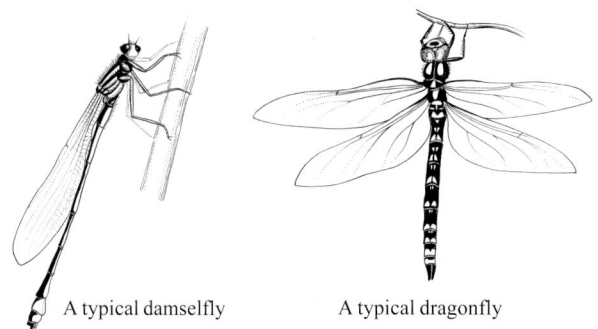

A typical damselfly   A typical dragonfly

The compound eyes of dragonflies and damselflies are divided into two sections. The upper part is very sensitive to ultraviolet light but apparently does not see colour and pattern very well, unlike the lower part which is able to perceive colour and pattern and seems to be used in identifying the suitability of potential prey. Insects flying above the dragonfly or damselfly are seen as a dark shape against a bright background. The animal climbs above its prey, stalling and then, if it is suitable, grabbing it with its specially adapted legs. Hawker dragonflies will also hunt ('hawk') around vegetation, searching for other insects resting on leaves or feeding on flowers.

This group of animals also has a unique method of reproduction. The male transfers sperm from reproductive organs at the end of the abdomen to accessory reproductive organs

Common blue damselfly [p15]

Dog's mercury flea beetles [p35]

Froghopper [p18]

Flat millipede [p39]

Horntail [p31]

Mayfly [p12]

Bug of Box Hill [p18]

Roesel's bush cricket [p16]

Hawthorn shieldbug [p18]

Banded demoiselle [p15]

Orange ladybird [p35]

Oak bush cricket [p16]

Parent bug and young [p18]

Southern hawkers paired [p15]

Robin's pincushion [p32]

at the front of the abdomen. When a suitable mate is found the male holds her by the back of the head, using claspers at the end of the abdomen; the female then inserts her reproductive organs into the male's accessory organs, forming a characteristic 'wheel'.

Damselflies can commonly be seen flying amongst vegetation along the banks of the River Mole.

Look out for

The Banded demoiselle *Calopteryx splendens* [p14]. The male of this species is metallic blue with dark bands on the wings; the female is metallic green with brown wings.

The Common blue damselfly *Coenagrion pulchellum* [p13].

There are many common dragonflies seen on Box Hill, again particularly by the river, although the larger species often hunt far from water.

Look out for

The Four-spotted chaser *Libellula quadrimaculata* [inside front cover], a fairly broad-bodied species often seen resting on tall plants by the water's edge.

The Southern hawker *Aeshna cyanea* [p14] often seen swooping along bankside trees and bushes. The males are mostly blue and the females greenish.

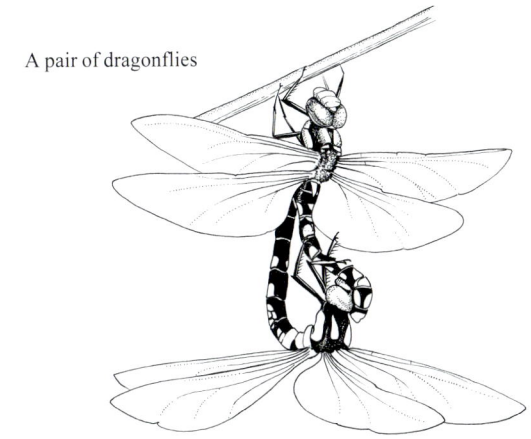

A pair of dragonflies

The Brown hawker *Aeshna grandis*, our largest dragonfly; its habits are similar to those of the previous species but its orange-brown wings are very distinctive.

STONEFLIES (order *Plecoptera*)

This is another order which has aquatic juveniles and the adults are rarely found far from water. They fly weakly and are usually found on tree trunks or low-growing vegetation close to the river. Short-lived, they feed on algae or lichens and have two long 'tails'.

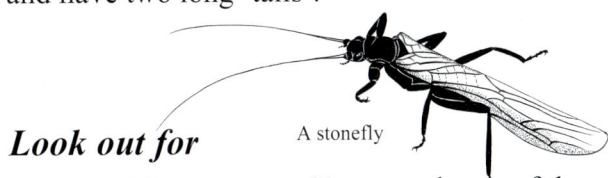

A stonefly

Look out for

Small brown stoneflies, members of the family *Leuctridae*, also known as 'pipe flies' or 'needle flies' because their wings are rolled round their body when they are at rest.

GRASSHOPPERS AND BUSH CRICKETS
(order *Orthoptera*)

These insects have hind legs which are enlarged for jumping. The size of the wings varies from species to species but some can fly well. The males of nearly all kinds attract their mates by making a high-frequency chirping noise (stridulation), produced by rubbing one part of the body against another.

Bush-crickets are easily distinguished from grasshoppers by their long antennae. Females also have a blade-like egg-laying organ (ovipositor). Grasshoppers are almost entirely herbivorous whilst some bush crickets are carnivorous.

Look out for

The Meadow grasshopper *Chorthippus parallelus*, our commonest species, which may be green, brown or even purple. The song is like 'a repeated short burst on a sewing machine'. This is our only flightless grasshopper; the female has both pairs of wings greatly reduced while the male has no hind wings. This is the most abundant species on rough grassy slopes like the Burford Spur.

A meadow grasshopper nymph

Two species which have always been common on Box Hill:

The Oak bush cricket *Meconema thalassinum* [p 14] which is common especially at dusk on a wide range of deciduous trees in the woodlands all over Box Hill, flies well and often comes to light at night. The male does not stridulate but drums on leaves and can apparently be heard several metres away.

A female Speckled bush cricket

The Speckled bush cricket *Leptophyes punctatissima*, a wingless species which is common on nettles, brambles and other scrubby vegetation, for example in Juniper Bottom and along the Military Road on the Burford Spur.

Two species which were formerly rare in Surrey but which are now common in some areas of the Hill, such as the long grass at the bottom of the Burford Spur and the open areas of Juniper Bottom:

The Long-winged conehead *Conocephalus discolor* [inside front cover] a slender species whose song is quiet, high-pitched and continuous.

Roesel's bush cricket *Metrioptera roeselii* [p13] a stubby species with a distinctive yellow edge to the top plate of the thorax, whose song resembles short bursts on a high-speed drill.

COCKROACHES (order *Dictyoptera*)

Closely related to Grasshoppers and Crickets, these are flattened, fast-running insects with long antennae. A number of introduced species have become notorious indoor vermin. However in Britain we have only three truly native outdoor living species.

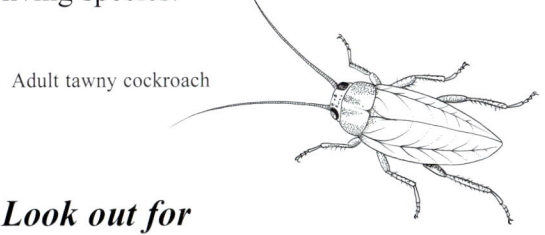
Adult tawny cockroach

Look out for

The **Tawny cockroach** *Ectobius pallidus*, a pale fawn animal up to 1cm long, in the long grass on Juniper Top and in Juniper Bottom.

EARWIGS (order *Dermaptera*).

These insects are recognised by the pair of pincers found at the end of the abdomen in adults. They are mainly ground-living and in the daytime are usually found in cracks or crevices or other dark places – a possible source of their name in folklore. They feed mainly on plant material. The forewings are very short; some species have no hind wings but if present these are elaborately folded beneath the short forewings and shaped like an earlobe – the other possible source of their name ('earwing' has become 'earwig'). Earwigs are reluctant to fly.

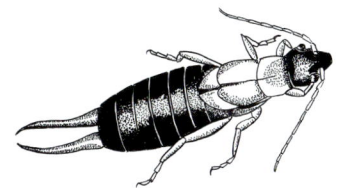
Female Common earwig

Look out for

The **Common earwig** *Forficula auriculata*, found in crevices in bark or under logs and stones in woodland or in rolled leaves on bushes. The female tends and protects her young when they are small.

TRUE BUGS (order *Hemiptera*)

There are three main groups of true bugs, distinguished from other insects by their segmented piercing, sucking mouthparts. Firstly, the suborder **Heteroptera** which includes plant bugs, damsel bugs and our largest land bugs, the shieldbugs (also known as 'stinkbugs' because when disturbed they give off unpleasant defensive smells). Secondly, the suborder **Homoptera**, which has two distinct groups, the **Auchenorryhncha,** including the froghoppers and leaf hoppers, mostly small but with one or two noticeable animals and the **Sternorrhyncha** —whitefly, scale insects and aphids, familiar garden pests.

Drawing showing piercing, sucking mouthparts

Look out for

The Hawthorn shieldbug *Acanthosoma haemorrhoidale* [p14] which is well camouflaged. Adults can be found in trees and bushes, where they feed on sap from leaves, in September and October and again from March to May after hibernation.

The grey and yellow Parent bug *Elasmucha grisea* [p14] which guards its eggs and then its young, protecting them from attack by parasites. Look out for it in late summer on birch leaves for example on the Military Road on the Burford Spur or on Mickleham Downs.

The formerly very rare 'Bug of Box Hill' *Gonocerus acuteangulus* [p13] which has spread from a very restricted area on the Zig Zag and is now found throughout Surrey with isolated records as far away as Brighton. It can be seen especially in the autumn and spring, before and after hibernation, sitting on low-growing vegetation in Juniper Bottom and on the lower slopes of the Burford Spur.

'Cuckoo spit' in the spring. This is the protective froth in which the young of the **Common froghopper** *Philaenus spumarius* [p13] lives. It is found all over Box Hill.

Cuckoo-spit

The large red-and-black froghopper *Cercopis vulnerata* [p13] which can be found in long grass and on bushes in May and June, for example in Juniper Bottom and on Mickleham Downs.

The beautifully camouflaged Tree hopper or **'Thorn hopper'** *Centrotus cornutus* [p28] whose thorax has thorn-like projections. The animal sits on the stems of bushes such as Dogwood, Wayfaring tree and Wild rose and can be seen on Juniper Top or Lodge Hill in spring or early summer.

A wingless aphid

Groups of Aphids on the stems of such plants as Wild rose, Stinging nettle or Knapweed by the sides of most paths on the Hill. They may be green ('greenfly') or black ('blackfly'). You may see large winged or wingless females giving birth to live young. Aphids pierce soft plant stems with their needle-like rostrum and suck up sap.

They excrete 'honeydew' which contains quite high concentrations of sugars and this is very attractive to ants – which 'herd' and 'milk' aphids, conferring protection from predators such as ladybirds and hoverfly larvae and parasites. Honeydew on leaves of trees is also very attractive to night-flying moths.

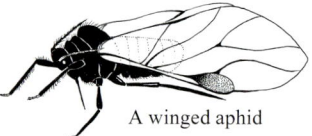

A winged aphid

Head of horsefly [p30]

Hoverfly [p30]

Wasp cranefly [p30]

Bee fly on primrose [p30]

St Mark's fly [p30]

Pale tussock caterpillar [p29]

Oak longhorn moth [p25]

Cinnabar moth larva [p29]

Poplar hawk moth larva [p26]

Elephant hawk moth larva [p26]

Elephant hawk moth adult [p26]

Cinnabar moth adult [p29]

Small elephant hawk moth [p26]

Hummingbird hawk moth [p26]

Peppered moth larva [p29]

Buff-tip caterpillars [p29]

Buff-tip adult [p29]

Marjoram moth on Marjoram [p25]

Privet hawk moth larva [p25]

Privet hawk moth adult [p26]

Small tortoiseshell larva with parasite cocoons [p33]

21

Cockchafer [p34]

Devil's coach-horse beetle [p34]

Eyed hawk moth larva with parasite grubs [p33]

Glow-worm larva and snail [p35]

Green woodpecker dropping [p32]

Rose chafer [p34]

THRIPS (order *Thysanoptera*)

These are most often noticed as minute black elongated insects on flowers where they scrape petal cells to obtain sap. Some species have long feathery wings and may swarm in their thousands in thundery weather – hence their names of 'thunder flies' or 'thunder bugs'.

Look out for

These insects looking like tiny elongated black specks in the flowers of Field or Hedge bindweed.

A thrip and an enlarged wing

LACEWINGS (order *Neuroptera*)

Most adults are green; a few are brown. All have delicate lace-like wings held over the back like a tent and very long antennae. The larvae are carnivorous, feeding on aphids and some species cover themselves in the remains of their prey as camouflage. The eggs are laid on long stalks, perhaps as a protection against ants which are associated with the aphids on which the larvae feed.

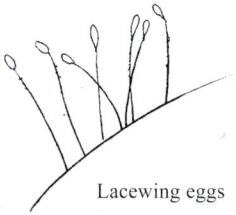
Lacewing eggs

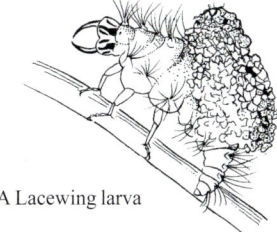
A Lacewing larva

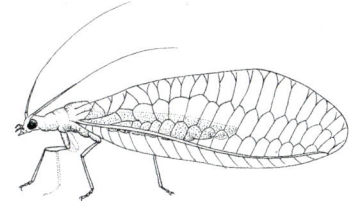
An adult common green lacewing

Look out for

The Common green lacewing *Chrysopa carnea* on trees and bushes in summer and in woodland for example on Ashurst Rough and in Juniper Bottom.

Chrysopa 7-punctata, **a bluish woodland species** with a black-spotted body which stinks horribly when picked up.

SNAKE-FLIES (order *Raphidioptera*)

These are closely related to Lacewings but have shorter antennae. The name comes from the long 'neck' which enables the insect to raise its head. The larvae live under tree bark and eat the young of other insects; the adults are aphid feeders.

A female snake-fly

Look out for

Snakeflies among trees or bushes in areas where there are dead trees whose bark provides the larval habitat – for example the Weypole, Juniper Bottom and Lodge Hill.

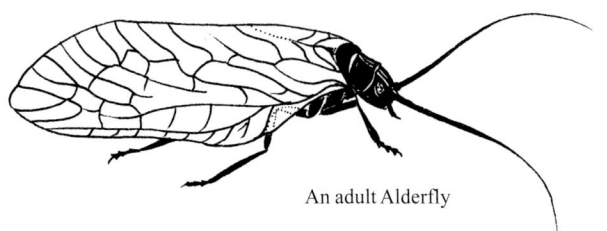

An adult Alderfly

ALDERFLIES (order *Megaloptera*)

Alderflies are another group with aquatic larvae which are carnivorous; the adults, which are like robust brown lacewings, do not feed. Eggs are laid on vegetation overhanging the river and the newly hatched larvae simply drop off into the water. The females will immerse themselves in the water if it is warmer than the air; this may speed up egg development.

Look out for

Adult Alderflies resting on long vegetation near the River Mole.

SCORPION FLIES (order *Mecoptera*)

Scorpion flies are scavengers eating other dead or dying insects or fruit, but will also drink nectar from flowers such as bramble. They have caterpillar-like larvae. The main distinguishing feature of the adult is the head which is pointed and beak-like; the mouthparts are at the end of a long 'face' which may help to keep the eyes clean when the insect is feeding on dead invertebrates. Males have an upturned end to the abdomen resembling the sting of a scorpion, from which they get their name. The wings are held flat above the body.

Look out for

The commonest of our scorpion flies, *Panorpa communis* [inside front cover], with its black-patterned wings, in spring and summer on low-growing bushes or on flowers in Juniper Bottom or by the river.

BUTTERFLIES AND MOTHS (order *Lepidoptera*)

Butterflies have been comprehensively covered in the *Box Hill Book of Butterflies* which also describes the common day-flying moths. However there are hundreds of species of night-flying moths on Box Hill. These include both the larger more frequently seen 'macros' and the far more numerous 'micros' (which although often minute – as small as 2mm across the wings – can be exquisitely coloured). Moths are an important food source for birds and bats, as well as being of interest because of the way in which they use colour to avoid predation.

We have selected a few species which you may come across almost anywhere on the Hill, flying by day, resting in low vegetation or on tree trunks, or flying round lights at night; or you may find their caterpillars, especially those of the large Hawkmoths, on trees and bushes.

Among the 'micros', look out for

The Oak longhorn *Adela reaumurella* [p19]; the males, which have iridescent green forewings and very long antennae, swarm round Oak trees on sunny days in spring and early summer. Females are similar but have much shorter antennae.

The Green oak tortrix *Tortrix viridiana* whose larvae hide in rolled Oak leaves and can be responsible for the large-scale defoliation of their foodplant. The pale green adults are common in oak woodland on the Hill in May and June.

The 'Grass moths' such as *Crambus culmellus* and *C. hamellus*, small creamy-white species which although night-flying are very abundant and easily disturbed from long grass during the daytime in the summer months. They rest head-down on grass stems where they are well-camouflaged.

The White plume moth *Pterophora pentadactyla*, a small white moth with feather-like wings, whose larvae feed on bindweed where the adults can be seen resting in the evening.

A White plume moth

The 'Marjoram moth' *Pyrausta purpuralis* [p21] a small (approx 1cm) triangular species often seen flying in daylight around its host plant.

LARGE MOTHS

Among the 'macros', the hawk moths are our largest and most spectacular species and on Box Hill there are seven resident and one frequent migrant species. Hawk moth caterpillars are most easily located by the damage done to their food plants – look out for shoots stripped of leaves or flowers. The adults, except for the Humming-bird hawk moth, rest during the day in well-camouflaged positions but can often be found when they have recently emerged and dried their wings, usually in the late afternoon or early evening. However these spectacular moths are in the minority – most 'macros' are much smaller and, at least superficially, brown or grey, but some species are regularly noticed.

Among the 'macros' look out for

The large apple-green caterpillars of the Privet hawk moth *Sphinx ligustri* [p21], with purple and white diagonal stripes and a black 'tail'. They can be found on Ash, Privet and Wayfaring trees between July and September – although they are large and spectacular they are often hard to find because of their camouflage. Look carefully on bushes at the sides of the grass slope on Juniper Top or on the Zig Zag slopes.

Larvae of the Poplar hawk moth *Laothoe populi* [p21] which are pale green with yellow diagonal stripes and a green 'tail'. They can be found in early summer and sometimes again in autumn, feeding on Willows and White poplars by the River Mole.

Larvae of the Large elephant hawk moth *Deilephila elpenor* [p20] which feed on Rosebay willowherb (Fireweed) and can often be seen climbing up the stems to feed early in the evening. You may also see them wandering on footpaths before pupation. They can be found anywhere on the Hill where Fireweed grows. This species has false eye spots on the front of the abdomen and, when it is feeding, the head and thoracic segments are stretched out, slightly resembling an elephant's trunk – hence the name 'Elephant hawk moth'. If disturbed the caterpillar retracts the head and the eye spots swell up; the caterpillar may even twitch the body from side to side (a threat display to deter predators) and is often mistaken for a small snake. The similar but smaller **Small elephant hawk moth** *Deilephila porcellus* feeds on bedstraws.

The beautiful pink adults [p20] of both species which are sometimes seen soon after emerging, sitting near patches of their respective food plants, or occasionally hovering around Honeysuckle flowers where they feed on the wing around dusk, between late May and early July.

The adults of the Privet hawk moth *Sphinx ligustri* [p26] which may be found late in afternoon or early evening, soon after emergence, sitting on fence posts.

The migrant Hummingbird hawk moth *Macroglossum stellatarum* [p20] which overwinters as an adult but until recently seemed unable to survive northern European winters. The moth migrates northwards in the spring and in 'good' years can arrive in April but is most frequently seen from mid-June onwards. The adult hovers in front of flowers – for example of Buddleia or Fuchsia – probing for nectar with its long tongue and if you are fortunate enough to be able to approach cautiously you may be able to see the moth flexing its 'tail' (in fact modified scales) and hear the audible hum of the wings. The caterpillar feeds on both Lady's and Hedge bedstraws in sunny positions on the downland slopes – for example below the viewpoint or on the Burford Spur and Juniper Top – and can be located by its habit of stripping flowering shoots.

As well as these more spectacular species look out for

Adults of the Ghost moth *Hepialus humuli*, the white males hover above long grass around dusk in late June/early July, often in small groups – this is known as 'lekking'. Females find the males by sight and collide with them, then mate.

Crab spider and prey [p36]

Funnel web spider [p36]

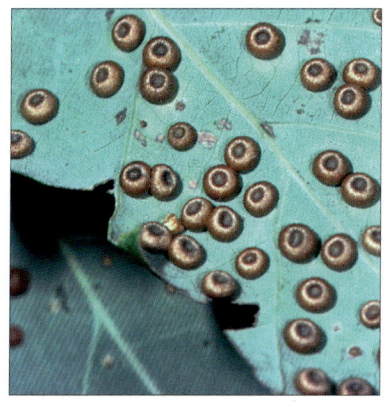
Silk button galls [p32]

Nail galls [p37]

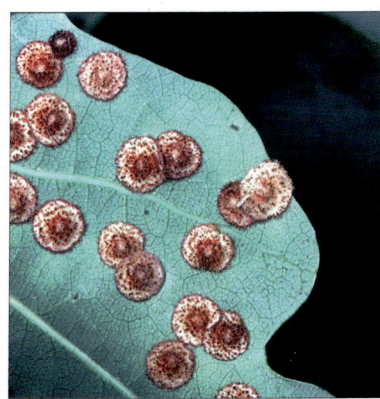
Spangle galls [p32]

Hazelnut weevil [p35]

Soldier beetles mating [p34]

27

Buff-tailed bumblebee [p34]

Lesser bloody-nosed beetle [p35]

Male bumblebee on thistle [p34]

Orb-web spider and dew [p36]

Worker bumblebee on Marjoram [p34]

Thorn hopper [p18]

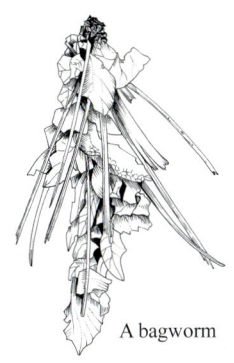
A bagworm

'Bagworms' (family *Psychidae*) whose larvae make cases, for example from twigs or bits of dead leaf. They may be found clinging to fence posts or tree trunks, where the larvae feed on algae and lichens, anywhere on the Hill.

Caterpillars of the Buff-tip moth *Phalera bucephala* [p21] which live gregariously on the shoots of Birch, Sallow and many other deciduous trees. They are black and yellow – warning colouration – and twitch violently when disturbed. They can occur almost anywhere on the Hill – look along woodland edges and wide rides. The adult [p21] is quite common but very rarely seen, as it is superbly camouflaged as a broken-off Birch twig.

The caterpillar of the Pale tussock or **Hop dog moth** *Calliteara pudibunda* [p19] which is pale green with two hairy 'horns', five white hair tufts on the back and a red 'tail'. It is often found wandering down tree trunks or on the ground before pupating in the autumn.

The Cinnabar moth *Tyria jacobeae* [p20] both caterpillars and adults are very obvious. The black and red adults, which resemble the Burnet moths, fly in May and June. The caterpillars [p20] have black and yellow stripes, and are common on ragwort in June and July, for example on Mickleham Downs.

Caterpillars of the Peppered moth *Biston betularia* [p21] which can be found especially on young Birch trees in late summer. They are stick-like and superbly camouflaged; the colour of an individual caterpillar is affected by chemicals in the leaves it eats, and those on Ash are quite different in colour from those on Birch, for example. The adults are rarely seen as they roost quite high up on tree branches, blending with lichens.

CADDIS FLIES (order *Trichoptera*)

Caddis flies are brownish insects with flimsy wings held tent-like over the back and covered with fine hairs. The long antennae are held out in front of the body when at rest. Our local species have aquatic larvae.

Look out for

Adults swarming over the water surface, or resting in long vegetation by the River Mole. They can however cover long distances and may be seen flying around lights.

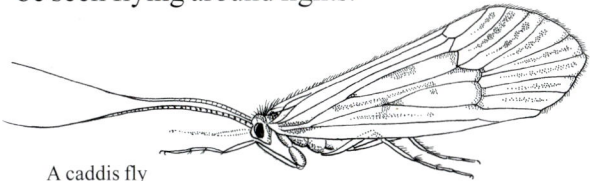
A caddis fly

29

TRUE FLIES (order *Diptera*)

True flies are distinguished by having one pair of developed wings (the forewings) and a pair of balancing organs – halteres. This is a very large and varied group of insects with an enormous range of lifestyles. It is impossible to do more than just touch on them.

Look out for

Craneflies or 'Daddy-long-legs'. The commonest species, *Tipula oleracea*, is the adult of the garden 'leatherjacket' which can be a pest.

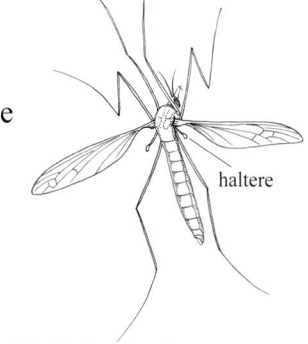

A typical cranefly ('Daddy-long-legs')

On Box Hill however the larvae feed on grass roots and the adults can be seen in long grass, for example on the Burford Spur. In woodland you may come across the spectacular wasp mimic *Nephrotoma crocata* [p19] whose larvae feed in damp leaf litter.

The non-biting midges – the Chironomids – whose larvae, which include the 'bloodworms' are aquatic. These often swarm over the river surface in enormous numbers or around trees and bushes in the evening.

The minute black biting midge (family *Ceratopogonidae*) — a real pest on a warm summer evening.

The St Mark's fly *Bibio marci* [p19], so named because it appears around St Mark's Day, 25th April, a black fly with long, dangling legs. Males are often seen swarming around trees and bushes in spring, waiting for females to emerge and fly upwards through the swarm. Although they look alarming they are completely harmless.

The horseflies or Clegs (family *Tabanidae*) [p19] which can be a real nuisance on warm humid days. They have mouthparts which resemble an electric carving-knife and the females pierce the skin, injecting anti-coagulants and histamines to encourage the flow of blood; this can cause a strong allergic reaction. The horsefly detects a potential food source partly by sight but also by changes in air temperature, humidity and carbon dioxide content. Males feed on flowers.

Bee flies (family *Bombylidae*) which hover in front of flowers such as primroses, violets and forget-me-nots in early spring; the commonest species on Box Hill is *Bombylius major* [p19]. The larvae live in bees' nests.

Hoverflies (family *Syrphidae*) which have a typical hovering, darting flight and mimic bees and wasps, from which they are distinguished by only having one pair of wings. The commonest species on Box Hill is the small orange-and-black *Episyrphus balteatus* [back cover] which can be seen nectaring in large numbers on the flower-heads of Hogweed and Wild parsnip in summer; the larvae eat aphids. Around buildings, especially in late summer, you may see large species such as *Volucella zonaria* [p19] which resemble bumblebees and whose larvae scavenge in the nests of bees and wasps. **Drone flies** such as *Eristalis tenax* [inside front cover] are often seen hovering along rides in woodland, their hind legs folded and dangling and giving the impression of being a honeybee's pollen basket.

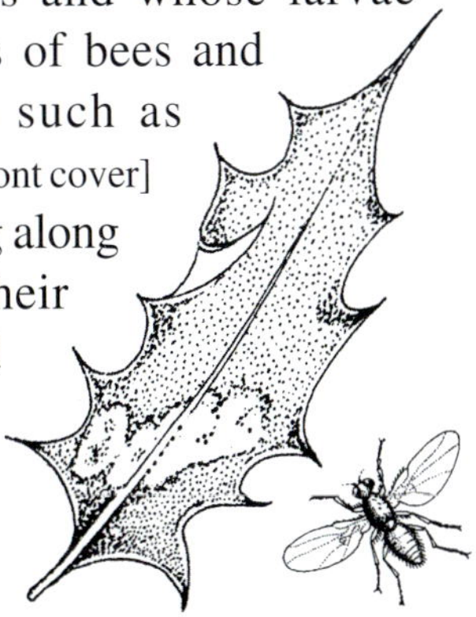

The Holly leaf miner
Phytomyza ilicis

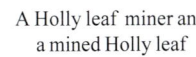
A Holly leaf miner and a mined Holly leaf

Although the minute adult Holly leaf miner is rarely seen, the damage caused to Holly leaves by the larvae is very obvious and few trees on the Hill escape infestation.

SAWFLIES, BEES, WASPS AND ANTS (order *Hymenoptera*)

Another enormously varied group of insects which is divided into two suborders, the **Symphyta** and the **Apocrita**.

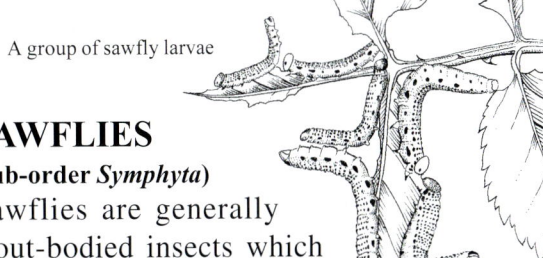
A group of sawfly larvae

SAWFLIES
(sub-order *Symphyta*)

Sawflies are generally stout-bodied insects which have no 'waist' between the thorax and the abdomen. The name 'sawfly' comes from the fact that the females of most kinds have a saw-like egg-laying organ, the ovipositor, which is used to cut slits in leaves or stems. In a few species the ovipositor is modified into a long sting-like organ. The larvae resemble caterpillars but differ from them in having more false legs or claspers (8 pairs) at the hind end. Caterpillars – the larvae of butterflies and moths – only have two, three or five pairs.

Look out for

Sawfly larvae living in clusters on wild rose or birch leaves; some kinds are green and yellow with black spots and twitch their tail ends in the air when disturbed – a collective defence mechanism.

Our largest sawfly, the Giant Horntail or **Wood wasp** *Uroceras gigas* [p13] which is black and yellow and, using its long ovipositor, drills into dead or dying Pine or Larch wood to lay its eggs.

BEES, WASPS AND ANTS
(suborder *Apocrita*)

Apocrita are distinguished from the Symphyta by having a typical wasp 'waist' between the thorax and the abdomen (although this may be hidden in hairy kinds such as bumblebees).

Gall wasps (family *Cynipidae*) are minute, often metallic insects, one of the groups of invertebrates which lay their eggs in leaves and flowers, accompanied by chemicals which result in deformed plant growth known as **galls**. These provide food for the larvae.

Look out for

'Robin's pincushion' [p14] on wild rose, caused by *Diplolepis rosae*.

Spangle and **silk button galls** [p27] on the leaves of Oak, caused by *Neuroterus* species.

Marble galls on Oak caused by *Andricus kollari*.

A marble gall

There are many other kinds of galls, caused by other gall wasps, mites and fungi – a full account of these is given in the new AIDGAP key (see reading list).

Ants (family *Formicidae*) are social insects whose large nests may be hidden underground, in or under logs, or may partly show as the familiar 'anthills' on chalk grassland. These nests can last for many years. Some species have an important mutual relationship with the blue butterflies such as the Adonis Blue *Polyommatus bellargus*.

Look out for

Anthills, especially in the grassland by the Zig Zag Road and on Juniper Top.

Abandoned anthills in areas recently colonised by woodland, for example in Juniper Bottom.

Green woodpeckers *Picus viridis* feeding on anthills and their droppings [p22], which consist almost entirely of ant exo-skeletons, on Juniper Top and in the fields next to the Zig Zag.

Ichneumon 'flies' (family *Ichneumonidae*) are just one of the many groups of parasitic Hymenoptera. Eggs are laid in or on the host (usually the larva of another insect, frequently the caterpillars of butterflies and moths, but sometimes a spider). The larvae fatally damage or kill the host before pupating. Female Ichneumons often have a very long sting-like ovipositor.

Look out for

Clusters of fluffy yellow cocoons on grass stems on the lower slopes of the Burford Spur or on Juniper Top – these have probably emerged from Burnet moth larvae – or on nettles where parasites have emerged from Small tortoiseshell larvae [p21].

Caterpillars such as those of Privet, Poplar or Eyed hawk moths or Peppered moth with parasite larvae burrowing out of the host [p22].

SOCIAL WASPS (family Vespidae)

Social wasps are easily recognised by their colouring but there are several very similar species to be found on Box Hill. Colonies are annual; in the autumn young queens emerge and mate, then hibernate in leaf litter or under logs. The colony from which they came disintegrates in early winter.

In the spring the mated females emerge from hibernation and build new nests. These are made of paper which first the queen, then the workers, produce by mixing chewed wood and saliva and are complex structures with a series of combs surrounded by protective walls. Nest temperature can be controlled to some extent by the workers. Adult wasps feed on nectar but also predate and eat other insects, and are important scavengers.

A queen Common wasp

Look out for

Streams of wasps emerging from underground nests (but take care not to approach too closely as wasps will defend their nests aggressively and sting).

In spring, queens and later workers scraping wood from the surface of fence posts and dead trees.

In summer, large holes where Badgers *Meles meles* **have excavated wasps' nests** to feed on the larvae and pupae; they seem to ignore stings! However any wasps which were away from the nest when it was destroyed may be extremely aggressive.

BEES

Bees include both social and solitary species. Most kinds are solitary, but may live in loose colonies with nests close together.

Look out for

The nests of solitary bees such as the **Tawny mining bee** *Andrena fulva*, [inside back cover] which makes holes in bare ground on the footpaths on the Burford Spur and Juniper Top.

33

The large **bumblebees** are colonial and the life-cycle is generally similar to that of the social wasps, although their combs are made of wax secreted by the queens and workers. Most species nest underground, often using abandoned bird or small mammal nests. Some species – the **cuckoo bees** – are parasitic and lay their eggs in bumblebee nests.

Look out for

Queen bumblebees such as the **Buff-tailed bumblebee** *Bombus terrestris* [p28] in spring on Sallow catkins or dandelions.

Worker bumblebees on flowers such as Bramble or Marjoram [p21] in the summer.

Male bumblebees on Bramble in late summer [p21]. These are more brightly coloured and in the black-and-yellow species have a yellow 'nose'.

BEETLES (order *Coleoptera*)

This is another huge order of insects with a wide range of different life styles. Most adults have two pairs of wings, the front pair being hardened and forming wing-cases (elytra) which protect both the body and, if they are present, the large folded membranous flying wings. There are some interesting and spectacular species on Box Hill.

Look out for

The Devil's coach-horse *Staphylinus olens* [p22], an unusual, ferocious-looking beetle which when threatened opens its large mandibles (jaws) and sticks its tail up in the air, producing an unpleasant smell. Again this is most often seen on woodland rides.

The Stag beetle *Lucanus cervus* [p1], the largest British beetle, is now rare on the Hill but is seen in most years. The male has enormous modified mandibles ('antlers') which it will use in 'fights' with other males but the female's mandibles are much smaller. The brown wing cases distinguish this from the smaller **Lesser stag beetle** *Dorcas parallelopipedus* which is much commoner.

Chafers which include the large brown **Maybug** or **Cockchafer** *Melolontha melolontha* [p21]. This often appears on warm evenings in May and June in and around woodlands. This brown beetle has distinctive black-and-white markings on the side of the abdomen and fan-like antennae. Another common chafer is the **Rose chafer** *Cetonia aurata* [p22], a large metallic green beetle which flies noisily round bramble and wild rose flowers in early summer, for example on Juniper Top or in Juniper Bottom.

Soldier beetles (family *Cantharidae*) [p27] are elongated orange or brown beetles which are often found congregating to mate and feed on the flowerheads of Wild parsnip or Hogweed in Juniper Bottom or on Mickleham Downs.

The Glow-worm *Lampyris noctiluca* which is most likely to be found in long grassland in early summer for example at the edge of the track in Juniper Bottom and by the Military Road on the Burford Spur. The larva [p22] predates snails such as the Banded snails and the common Garden snail (*Helix* species), injecting poisons and digestive enzymes into its victim, then eating them. Fully-grown female Glow-worms resemble the larvae, having no wings or wing-cases, and attract males by emitting a greenish glow from the rear end of the abdomen. The winged males also emit a glow. Sadly, the Glow-worm is far less common than it once was, but it can still be seen on warm evenings in summer.

Ladybirds which are well represented on Box Hill. Like most species, the **Two-spot** and **Seven-spot ladybirds** *Adalia bipunctata* and *Coccinella 7-punctata* and their larvae feed on aphids. They can be seen on bushes and flowers almost anywhere on the Hill.

However, the **Orange ladybird** *Halyzia 16-guttata* [p14] whose first Surrey record was at Juniper Hall in 1986, eats the mildew growing on aphid honey-dew on broad-leaved trees such as Sycamore. It is common in woodland on Mickleham Downs and Lodge Hill.

A Seven-spot ladybird eating an aphid

The **Lesser bloody-nosed beetle** *Timarcha goettingensis* [p28] which is often found trundling around in the short turf of chalk grassland, for example on the Zig Zag. It can produce red fluid from its mouthparts when annoyed – a defence against predators.

Weevils (family *Curculionidae*) are relatively small beetles with elbowed antennae, often borne on an extension to the front of the head (the rostrum). The **Nettle weevil** *Phyllobius urticae* [front cover] is a beautiful green species which can commonly be seen on nettles in Juniper Bottom in the spring. The female of the **Hazelnut weevil** *Curculio nucum* [p27] uses the mouthparts at the end of her very long rostrum to pierce young hazelnuts and lay an egg in each nut. You may find fallen hazelnuts with a small neat round emergence hole.

The Dog's mercury flea beetle *Hermeophaga mercurialis* [p13]. If you approach Dog's mercury plants, in Juniper Bottom or on Mickleham Downs, quietly in the spring you should be able to see this tiny black beetle but as soon as it is disturbed it jumps down into the vegetation. By midsummer the beetle and its larvae will have reduced many Dog's mercury leaves to lace.

Animals whose adults have eight jointed legs

SPIDERS, HARVESTMEN, TICKS AND MITES (class *Arachnida*)

SPIDERS (order *Araneae*)

These are distinguished from other Arachnids by having a narrow 'waist' between the thorax and an unsegmented abdomen. They have the ability to spin silk threads from spinnerets at the hind end of the abdomen. Some species spin complex webs, others use their silk threads as lifelines and all produce a cocoon in which the eggs are hidden.

Look out for

The webs of the orb-weavers (family *Araneidae*) [p28] which includes the **Garden cross spider** *Araneus diadematus*. These are especially obvious on dewy mornings in the early autumn, in low-growing bushes.

The funnel webs of spiders of the family *Agelenidae* (usually *Agelena labyrinthica*) [p27] among low shrubs and in long grass in Juniper Bottom or on Mickleham Downs.

Crab spiders (family *Thomisidae*) which are often brightly coloured and hide in flowers where they are camouflaged from both predators and potential prey. The commonest of these, *Misumena vatia* [p27], can be white or yellow, depending on which flowers it hides in. A white specimen can slowly change to yellow owing to the expansion of pigment cells in the cuticle (skin). It is often seen on the flower heads of Wayfaring tree and Ox-eye daisy wherever these grow on the Hill.

Wolf Spiders (family *Lycosidae*), fast moving, ground-running hunters often found amongst leaf litter on the woodland floor or in the grassland, feeding on insects and other spiders. Females may be carrying egg cases, held by their spinnerets or carrying young on their back [inside back cover].

A typical Harvestman

Harvestmen (order *Opiliones*)

These differ from spiders in having no 'waist' – the head, thorax and abdomen are fused into one unit – and in having visible segments on the abdomen. In most species the legs are very long and the eyes are borne on a 'wart' on top of the head. They feed on dead or dying invertebrates.

Look out for

Our commonest species, *Leiobunum rotundum*, resting on tree trunks or leaves low down in the vegetation.

MITES AND TICKS (order *Acari*)

Most mites and ticks are very small (less than 2mm) but a few species are noticeable because of the effects they have on plants and mammals (including dogs and humans). They can be distinguished from spiders in not having a 'waist and from the harvestmen by the absence of visible segments.

They exhibit a wide range of different life styles. Some free living species are mainly plant feeders or feed on organic debris. Others are carnivores, mainly feeding through scavenging or by parasitism, at least at some stage of their life cycle. Ticks, for example, although spending most of their time amongst vegetation, attach themselves to a vertebrate host when they need to feed on its blood.

Look out for

The red velvet mite *Trombidium holosericeum*, a bright red carnivore, it can be found crawling among low vegetation.

Mites hitching rides on other invertebrates, for example on the undersides of bees and beetles.

Small red parasitic mites on the legs of harvestmen or the bodies of butterflies such as the Large skipper *Ochlodes venata* [inside back cover].

Red 'nail galls', up to 1cm long, on the upper surface of the leaves of Sycamore, These are caused by *Aceria macrorhynchus* [p27].

Beware of

The Harvest mite *Trombicula autumnalis* which can reach a size of 4 mm but, in its smaller stages (so small that it is invisible to the naked eye), can be a real nuisance. It is abundant on chalk grassland in late summer and autumn, its bite causing severe itching especially where clothing is tight. Although not dangerous it can be extremely irritating.

The sheep tick *Ixodes ricinus* [inside back cover]. There are several kinds of ticks on Box Hill but this is the species you are most likely to encounter – probably on your dog after a walk on the Hill. Females sit among long vegetation and detect the approach of a suitable host by vibrations. They then crawl onto the host and pierce the skin, sucking blood which they need in order to be able to produce fertile eggs. As they feed the body swells to the size of a small grape before it finally detaches itself and drops off. Ask your vet for a special tool which will easily remove these.

Animals whose adults have more than eight jointed legs

WOODLICE

(**class** *Crustacea* **order** *Isopoda*)

All five of the common woodlouse species are to be found on Box Hill. Most woodlice are nocturnal and hide under logs and in leaf litter during the daytime. They are related to aquatic shrimps and still breathe by means of gills and therefore need to keep damp. Pill woodlice however are able to conserve moisture by rolling into a ball and are therefore more likely to be seen moving around in grassland during the daytime. Young are carried in brood pouches to prevent them drying out.

There is much folklore associated with woodlice. Stephen Hopkin, in the AIDGAP key [p40], refers to a recipe for woodlouse sauce (Holt 1885); they have been used as a remedy for stomach-aches and other minor ailments and have a number of endearing common names such as 'chiggypigs' and 'cheeselogs'.

They rarely cause significant damage to living plants, feeding mainly on dead plant material; they are an important part of the woodland food cycle, breaking down large pieces of organic matter, thus promoting fungal and bacterial decomposition.

Woodlice have an ill-deserved reputation as pests mainly because they are often found in houses, where they have retreated to avoid supersaturation in wet weather.

Look out for

The Common shiny woodlouse *Oniscus asellus* and the **Common rough woodlouse** *Porcellio scaber* which hide in leaf litter or under logs in woodland, coming out to feed and often climbing tree trunks in the evening

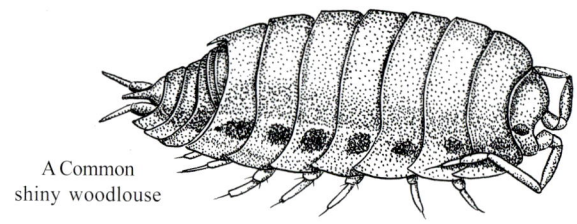

A Common shiny woodlouse

The Common pill woodlouse *Armadillidium vulgare* [inside back cover] which can be seen trundling around on the chalk grassland on Juniper Top and the Burford Spur.

Pill woodlice can be distinguished in several ways from Pill millipedes which are described on the next page. Pill woodlice are rarely seen on the acid clay cap of the Hill and are very active on warm days. They soon unroll from their protective position. Pill millipedes on the other hand are very secretive and conceal themselves under logs in damp places. Pill woodlice have only 14 legs, one pair per segment, while pill millipedes have 38 legs, with 2 pairs per segment. When rolled up these two species have differently-shaped armour plates at the hind end.

A curled-up pill woodlouse

A curled-up pill millipede

CENTIPEDES (Class *Chilopoda*)

These animals are carnivorous with claws at the head end. These are used to grab their prey which is then immobilised by poison from glands situated at the base of the claw. There are two main groups living on Box Hill.

Look out for

The fast-running orange surface hunters (lithobiomorphs) in woodland leaf litter. They have long legs, enabling them to travel at speed and search visually for prey.

The blind burrowing species (geophilomorphs) which are long and thin with short legs and flexible bodies, adapted to crawling through the soil to catch their prey.

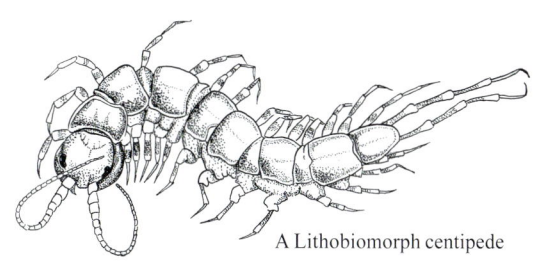
A Lithobiomorph centipede

MILLIPEDES (Class *Myriapoda*)

Millipedes can be distinguished from centipedes by the absence of claws at the head end and by having two pairs of legs per segment as against one pair per segment in the centipedes. All millipedes are scavengers, mainly eating dead plant material. There are three main groups on Box Hill; flat, snake and pill millipedes.

Look out for

The flat millipedes (Polydesmids) resting under logs [p13].

The snake millipedes (Iulids) [inside back cover] which coil up like a watch spring when disturbed. If observed carefully and quietly they will uncoil and walk away. Notice how the legs move in 'waves'.

The pill millipede *Glomeris marginata* [inside back cover] which looks and behaves quite like the pill woodlouse but has no narrow segments on its rear end and has far more legs. It can take 11 to 12 years to mature as it eats dead wood which has very low energy and nutrient contents.

Further reading and references

If you wish to investigate invertebrates in more detail then we suggest the following publications:

At a popular level, there is a series of excellent Field Studies Council (FSC) foldout charts, which are available from Juniper Hall Field Centre (Telephone: 0845 458 3507): these include:

    Bebbington & Bebbington (2003). *A Guide to Bugs on Bushes.* FSC Occasional Publication no. 77.

    Bebbington, Bebbington & Tilling (1994). *The Woodland Name Trail.* FSC Occasional Publication no. 32.

    Bebbington & Lewington (2002). *A Guide to the Caterpillars of the Butterflies of Britain and Ireland.* FSC Occasional Publication no. 70.

    Bebbington & Lewington (1998). *A Guide to the Butterflies of Britain.* FSC Occasional Publication no. 48.

    Bee & Lewington (2002). *A Guide to House and Garden Spiders.* FSC Occasional Publication no. 69.

    Brooks & Askew (1999). *A Guide to the Dragonflies and Damselflies of Britain.* FSC Occasional Publication no. 53.

    Hopkin (2003). *The Woodlouse Name Trail.* FSC Occasional Publication no. 75.

    Marshall & Ovenden (1999). *A Guide to British Grasshoppers and allied Insects.* FSC Occasional Publication no. 54.

At a more advanced level the FSC's AIDGAP project publishes a series of identification keys, which are also available from Juniper Hall Field Centre. These include:

    Hopkin (1991) *A key to the woodlice of Britain and Ireland.*
        Reprinted from *Field Studies* vol. 7 no. 4. ISBN 1 85153 204 8.

    Jones-Walters (1989). *Keys to the families of British spiders.*
        Reprinted from *Field Studies* vol. 7 no. 2. ISBN 1 85153 197 1.

Lace border moth
Scopula ornata

Plant (1997). *A key to the adults of British lacewings and their allies.* Reprinted from *Field Studies* vol. 9 no. 1. ISBN 1 85153 201 3.

Redfern & Shirley (2002). *British plant galls; identification of galls on plants and fungi.* Reprinted from *Field Studies* vol. 10 no. 2 and 3.   ISBN 1 85153 214 5.

Unwin (2001). *A key to the families of British bugs (Insecta, Hemiptera).* Reprinted from *Field Studies* vol. 10 no. 1. ISBN 1 85153 212 9

Recommended books:

Chinery (1986). *Collins guide to the insects of Britain and western Europe.* HarperCollins. ISBN 0 00 219137 7

Jeffcoate (2002) *The Box Hill Book of Butterflies.* The Friends of Box Hill. ISBN 0 9 534430 4 3

Townsend & Waring (2003) *Field Guide to the Moths of Great Britain and Ireland.* British Wildlife Publishing.

There is also an excellent series of *Naturalists' Handbooks* published by the Richmond Publishing Company. The 28 titles to date include many of relevance to this book and can be bought from the Juniper Hall shop (0845 458 3507) or direct from Richmond Publishing (01703 643104).

No attempt has been made to reflect the relative sizes of the animals in the drawings and photographs which appear in this book.

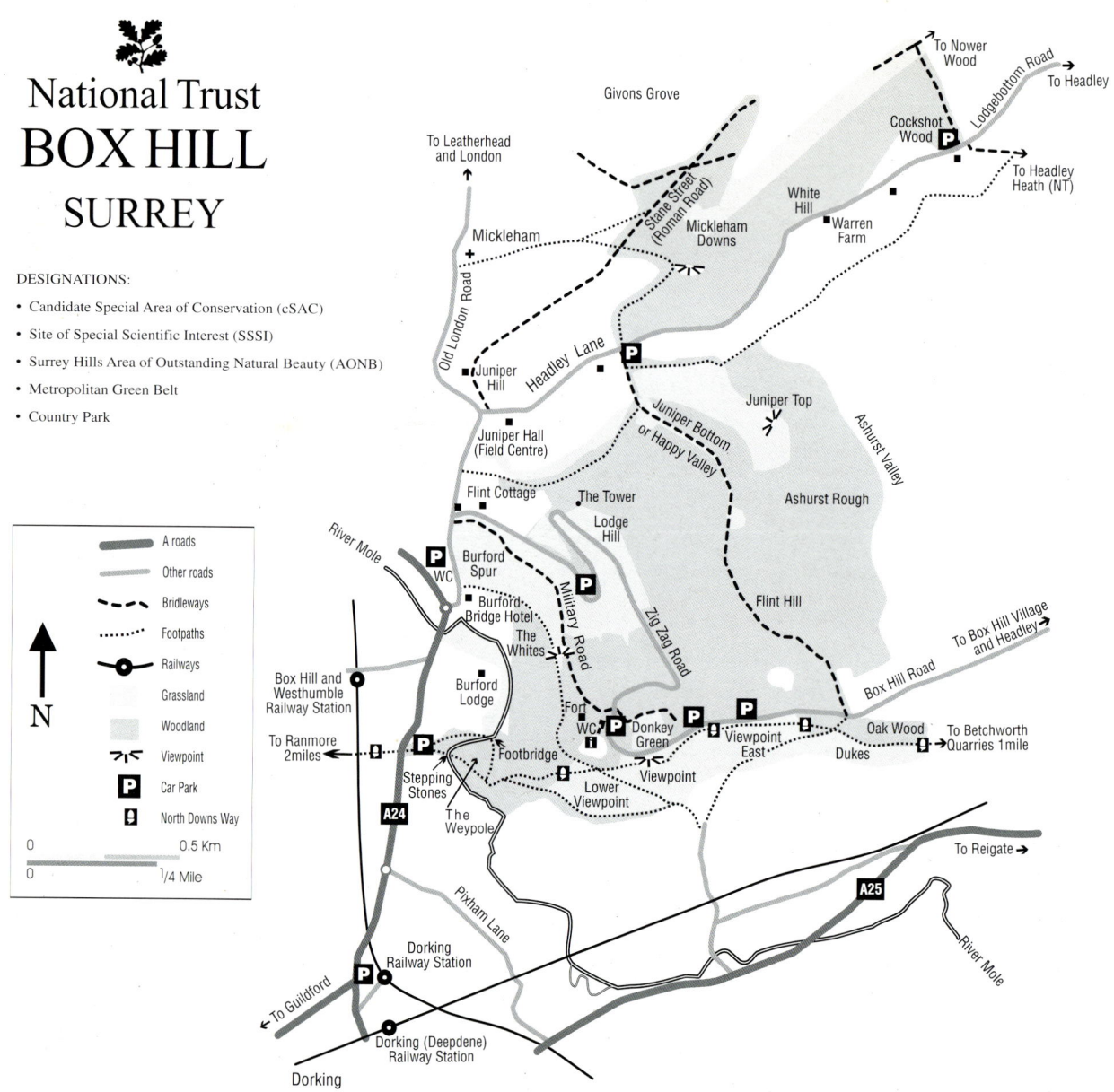